Heart of the Country

JEREMY MOORE & WILLIAM CONDRY

HEART OF THE COUNTRY

GOMER

First Impression
2003

ISBN 1 84323 203 0
ISBN 1 84323 276 6 (Hardback)

This book is published with the support of the Arts Council of Wales.

Thanks are also due to the Editor of *The Guardian* for permission to
use the *Country Diary* entries included in this book.

Printed in Wales by Gomer Press, Llandysul, Ceredigion

PREFACE

The Heart of the Country reminds us anew that the beauty of landscape can be appreciated in many different ways. This venture offers a stunning combination of visual image and thought-provoking description and debate. The writer, William Condry, shared with his readers his knowledge, his principles and his great love for wildlife; photographer Jeremy Moore gives us new insights into the shapes, the seasons and the character of the land itself. I consider myself privileged indeed to have been born in a part of Wales where there is majesty in the landscape and solitude to be found for those who wish to observe the natural world. This book celebrates the innumerable places in Wales where that is still the case: in the curve of a river, the slope of a woodland bank, sunlight on an estuary or a bird in flight, William Condry and Jeremy Moore have found cause to wonder and give praise. Long may other visitors to Wales enjoy and appreciate this beauty. As the writer himself asserts: we have in Wales 'as generous a slice of unspoilt nature as you can hope to find anywhere in the world today.'

Mae prydferthwch tirlun Cymru yn destun rhyfeddod ledled y byd. Diolch felly am gyfrol sy'n ein hatgoffa, yn ymwelwyr neu frodorion, am yr harddwch oesol hwnnw sy'n cuddio ymhob cwm a chilfach. Boed yng ngeiriau craff William Condry neu yn ffotograffau ysblennydd Jeremy Moore, dyma ddathliad swmpus ac ystyrlon o ffurfiau a chymeriad tymhorau'r tir. Fy mraint i oedd cael fy magu yng nghwmni'r unigeddau mewn ardal a gynigiai gyfoeth i'r sawl a garai fyd natur yn ei holl ogoniant. A dyna yw cynnig tirlun Cymru benbaladr o hyd. Dewch felly i werthfawrogi haf a gaeaf yr afon, yr hebog ar wib yr awelon; machlud hir dros dir neu don, a moelydd yr ymylon. Dewch, gyda'r awdur a'r ffotograffydd, i ryfeddu.

Jonathan Jones
(Bwrdd Croeso Cymru/Wales Tourist Board)

It could be said that I owe the existence of this book to a piece of music. William Condry's memorial service had ended with Vaughan Williams's 'A Lark Ascending', and in summer 2001 I unexpectedly heard that wonderful piece again. In a truly emotional response my feelings about him returned. The truth is I had been far more affected by his life and his death than those of my own father. It was also a rare moment of clarity and it gave me the impetus to go forward with my idea for this book.

I had known Bill since 1980, when he was warden of the Ynys-hir RSPB reserve, near Machynlleth. Inspired by his 'New Naturalist' book about the Snowdonia National Park, and anxious to meet him, I offered to do voluntary work on the reserve. On my first visit he took me to listen to the reed warblers which had recently arrived on the Dyfi estuary, and then left me to work with a billhook on some conifers. Within a few minutes I had sliced my thumb open and had to find my own way to hospital.

Despite the inauspicious first encounter, I met Bill from time to time at Ynys-hir and elsewhere. Though there was a huge difference in age, experience and knowledge between us, I felt that we seemed to speak the same language. If he disliked the human race en masse, he had a rare ability to communicate on a personal level with humour, intelligence and respect.

He was an old-school naturalist motivated by a genuine love and enthusiasm for wildlife which had begun early in childhood. An education in the arts ensured that his perception of his surroundings was never blinkered by the scientific method. I can't recall an exact *number* of birds, for example, being mentioned in any of his Diaries. What comes over instead is their beauty, their interest and their importance. This appreciation of nature's glories would became in turn an environmental mission. For Bill will also be remembered as one of the father figures of conservation in the UK - thanks to his dedication in their early days to the Red Kite Committee, the

Bardsey Island Bird Observatory and the West Wales Field Society. Even in his old age he supported new conservation initiatives: in 1989 I was one of a group of people who set up Friends of Cardigan Bay to promote marine conservation off the west Wales coast, and Bill kindly agreed to become our figurehead.

As a writer, he was able to communicate quite complex ideas in a deceptively simple style. As well as classic books on Wales and its natural history, and other subjects, Bill was widely known for his 'Country Diaries' which appeared fortnightly in *The Guardian* between 1957 and his death. Many were descriptions of places and wildlife, while others were of a more philosophical nature. Almost every one was a gem in its own way, many having a sting in the tail. Never in the very last sentence, for he had learned by experience that if the punchline was right at the end, it was liable to be cut!

He also used his *Guardian* column to bring conservation issues to the attention of a wider public. He could be extremely outspoken – for example in the first piece here – but this was the result of genuine anger at the relentless loss of wildlife he saw going on around him. It is clear from his Diaries that he recognised these losses at an early stage. At first his voice may have been a solitary one but during his lifetime conservation become a powerful force in the countryside. He would have seen forestry policy, for example, become more wildlife friendly. It is only since his death, however, that there have been genuine changes in agriculture – and even then, one suspects, reluctantly.

During his life I was not able to collaborate with Bill professionally. He did, however, agree to write a foreword to an earlier version of my first book *Wales - the Lie of the Land*, which never saw the light of day. It was through his contacts with Gomer Press in Llandysul, though, that it was eventually published. 'I strongly advise you,' he told me, 'to approach them with your ideas'. So I owe a debt to him personally, but far more than that we all owe a debt to him for his descriptions of Wales and its wildlife and the simple beauty of his writing.

It is to my regret that I knew him so poorly and spent so little time with him. Here was a pioneer in the world of conservation who, together with his wife, Penny, actually put his 'green' ideals into practice. We will probably never know the nitty-gritty of his career as writer or conservationist, or his relationships with his fellows. 'The story of my unadventurous life would not be of the slightest interest to anybody,' he writes in the preface to his autobiography, published in 1995. It is frustratingly short on personal details, so perhaps, like the book's title, *Wildlife, My Life* was a genuine reflection of his nature.

Bill's 'Country Diaries' now form part of his Archive at the National Library of Wales in Aberystwyth, and total about a thousand separate pieces. Selection for this book was a formidable task. I excluded those which had already appeared in *A Welsh Country Diary* and others because they directly promoted a book, organisation or meeting. Others I left out because they covered topics which I could not tackle photographically - many wildlife subjects, for example. I made a list of those which I thought might work, and began to search for relevant images in my files. At the same time I began to visit locations Bill had written about. The temptation was to illustrate a place or feature exactly but I soon found that a more creative and fruitful solution was to take a sideways glance at his themes and see what emerged. The best images were sometimes the unexpected ones. Towards the end of the project, continually frustrated by dismal weather, it was a real thrill to find a new 'match' between image and text.

There is probably a bias towards Bill's more campaigning pieces in this book. Conservation is often about land-use – a subject that particularly interests me as a photographer. Readers may be surprised about some of the schemes Bill mentions. I knew nothing about proposals for a road around Pumlumon, a giant reservoir in the upper Elan valley, or open-cast mining in the Mawddach valley, until I began my research. There can be little doubt that Bill's highlighting of these schemes contributed to their rejection. Here was a man who really made a difference.

I must thank several people for their help. Firstly, Penny Condry, who was supportive from the word go, and without whom the project would not have gone ahead. Secondly, Arthur Chater, botanist and great friend of the Condrys, who was a mine of information on the plants of Ceredigion.

Then I would like to thank National Nature Reserve wardens Mike Bailey, Hywel Roberts and Arfon Hughes for their advice, and Ian and Cath Callan, who showed me their magnificent flower meadow. Thanks also to Mairwen Prys Jones, Francesca Rhydderch and Ceri Wyn Jones of Gomer Press, to Elgan Davies for the book's elegant design and to Jane Powell for help with editing. My thanks also go to the Arts Council of Wales for their support, and particularly Bryn Jones; and lastly to Will Troughton and other National Library of Wales staff for their invaluable assistance.

Bill spent the last forty years of his life in a remote farmhouse on the saltmarshes of the Dyfi estuary, not far from Machynlleth, and it was this town's name which prefaced almost all his 'Country Diaries'. Jan Morris describes in 'A Machynlleth Triad' how the town is, both historically and geographically, truly at the heart of Wales. So this book's title refers to the place where Bill's home had been for half his lifetime, but in a way it also describes the man himself. It is an honour that my own work can now be seen alongside his.

Jeremy Moore, April 2003

HERE WE LIVE between two famous mountains, Plynlimon and Cader Idris. Plynlimon is a vast bulge of wild moorland, now threatened by a deplorable scheme to improve it for farming. Cader Idris in contrast is higher and rockier and is, or should be, protected by being in a national park. But even Cader has recently suffered. One of its flanks has been horribly scarred by new farm roads which run by the slopes and can be seen as eyesores from far away. The fact is that if you are a farmer, you are no ordinary mortal. Without planning permission you can erect the most unbeautiful buildings. And you can make roads wherever you like and as ugly as you like. Then as a reward you collect marvellous grants from that nonsensical EEC. Pressure groups of farmers and foresters have long had their hearts set on the exploitation of the uplands. In this they are encouraged by sweeping statements from the Countryside Commission, such as: 'Everyone concerned about the uplands can agree on the need to develop the economic life of the uplands.' This is just not true. Everyone does not agree. Take sheep farming, for instance. Some of us fail to see the point of increasing upland sheep production because on such poor land it can never be successful without vast subsidies. In any case we can easily do without the additional produce. Leave the uplands as they are, some of us say, or let them get wilder. As the population grows and the world of micro-chips and televisions begins to drive us all mad, we are going to need our wildnerness areas more and more.

The foothills of Pumlumon, Ceredigion.

WE CHOSE A BAD DAY for our botanical frolic on the heights of Moelwyn. After weeks of dry weather the uplands suddenly retreated into the clouds and we found ourselves in thick fog at only 500 ft. At 1,500 ft there was rain, and wind as well, as we pressed on upwards, steering only by a compass. A wall of naked cliffs loomed out of the fog, but where was the Alpine plant we sought? All about us we saw little but parsley fern which, as a resolute hater of limestone, indicates those rocks least likely to be a haven for a wealth of other plants. Had we come all that way, in this weather, at some cost of weariness, to find only parsley fern? This mountain venture was a real pilgrimage. We were seeking what in Wales is a very local plant, the northern rock-cress, first found on Moelwyn three centuries ago by the pioneer Welsh botanist, Edward Lhuyd. Eventually, after groping up to the summit to get our bearings and down again to the cliffs, we found our rock-cress, its little white, four-petalled blooms not the most striking flowers in the world but deeply satisfying to us. It was not in delirious abundance but we were happy to see that there was far more of it than we had dared to hope. As we left the cliffs for the open shoulders of the mountain, the clouds began to lift, then soon unravelled completely. The mist disappeared and we looked round at vast expanses of the uplands, from Snowdon in the north to the diminishing hills of the Llŷn peninsula in the west, with Bardsey Island visible beyond the land. Below us lay the Glaslyn valley which until William Madocks built his ugly embankment in 1811 was a beautiful estuary. Would he, we wondered, have got planning permission for such a monstrosity today? As we came home, past that nuclear power station in the heart of a national park, we could see that the answer was yes, he probably would.

Blaenau Ffestiniog and Trawsfynydd nuclear power station.

A MARVELLOUS PLANT is ivy, especially now when, while most other plants are past flowering, ivy is just at its best. Let the sun shine and bees, wasps, butterflies, hoverflies and others gather at this last nectar treat of the year; and on one exciting occasion I even saw the rare large Tortoiseshell butterfly at ivy flowers in October. But come the gloom of November and many insects vanish into the shadows of the very green ivy leaves. So next time you feel impelled to cut down any ivy it might be as well to remember that you may be destroying the winter quarters of butterflies as choice as Brimstone, Peacock, Tortoiseshell and Holly Blue. You may also be destroying a chief food of the birds. For in late winter many blackbirds, redwings and other thrushes rely much on ivy berries to get them over a difficult few weeks. Then spring arrives and ivy becomes a chief concealment for nests. It is because it is so heavily mantled in ivy that one of my favourite medieval castles has such a marvellous atmosphere of mystery. But I hear it is to be restored and opened to the public. All the ivy, of course, will be cleared away. There will be a large coach and car park and thousands of people will visit it every year. I shall not be among them. I shall prefer to remember it as it was: a splendid though unintentional nature reserve.

Near Devil's Bridge, Ceredigion.

WE LIVE IN AN AGE of conferences. Some, I suppose, are a waste of time. But others, like the one I went to last week organised by the Campaign for the Protection of Rural Wales, have a real message. Its subject was a large one, no less than the future of the coast of Wales; and as our meeting was at New Quay in Cardiganshire, one of our concerns was Cardigan Bay which will be threatened by gross pollution if oil is ever struck there. After the conference I took the cliff path out to the breezy heights of New Quay Head which gave me a panorama of the whole of this beautiful bay which has survived for thousands of years as a haven for seals, dolphins, porpoises and a multitude of fish and seabirds. In the south-west, I could see the coast all the way down to St David's Head. In the north were all those Caernarfonshire hills that march out into the sea in one long beautiful line. Choughs played in the wind about me. Far below me, five black shags stood on a rock amid deep green water. Just above me hovered a kestrel. Just below me hovered another. Far away over the sea gleaming white gannets dived repeatedly into the water from great height. It was a perfect scene, but I could not help wondering, in view of what I had just heard at the conference, whether I was looking at yet another part of the planet that man is about to ruin. I walked back to my car and drove home, fully aware that the petrol in my tank might have come from the spoilation of some spot in the world which had once been just as lovely as Cardigan Bay. But that is no argument for further vandalism. Some places, even if they are rich in oil, should be sacrosanct. Would-be exploiters need to be resisted in all such precious places.

Oiled common scoter, Marros, Carmarthenshire.

THE EAST WINDS do blow and as we wonder what's coming next we think back to those awesome winters that stand along the years of our lives like milestones. What about that unforgettable freeze-up that lasted from mid-December 1962 until mid-January 1963? When it was over we all compared it with January and February 1947 and the general feeling was that the snows of 1947 had been heavier but that the frosts of 1962-63 were more severe. Both winters were immensely destructive of wildlife, but what singled out 1962-63 as exceptionally cruel was the phenomenal mortality of shellfish. Along the coast of Cardigan Bay the sea froze along its margins and the frost was hammered deep into sandy beaches by the north-east wind, killing incredible numbers of star fish, crabs, razor shells, prickly cockles and the little fishes called gobies. Millions of creatures were washed up dead and lay along the tide line for weeks. Only crows and gulls were happy. Other birds were sorely stricken, especially mistle thrush, starling, redwing, wren, long tailed tit, heron and some other water birds. Our local ducks and geese had to take to the open sea when the estuary became completely covered with ice floes. Someone found a bittern that was dying and two choughs that were already dead. After every dreadful winter mother nature sets about stitching the world together again and in a few years even the most decimated species usually recover their numbers. But amongst the birds there was one loss in 1962-63 which even now has not been made good. To say goodbye to the wood lark, to my ears the most accomplished singer of them all, remains a real sadness.

Glandyfi, Ceredigion.

IT WAS AT THIS TIME of year that I once heard a Welsh hills farmer use the expressive word *hirlwm* which I am told might be translated as 'the long bareness'. It refers to the bleak depressing look of the upland pastures in winter when so much of the mountain grass is white in death and useless to the sheep. The word came to my mind a few days ago as I walked over one of the great curving shoulders of Cader Idris in a world of thick cloud and cold squalls of hail. Up there I could detect very few signs of life, not so much as a raven, a crow or even a sheep.

Though it was mid-winter I looked for Alpine plants but at first saw nothing except the mosses and lichens which defy all rain, all cold and every wind that blows. I scrambled higher and began to find some of those mountain plants that will be a glory of next summer but which were now in the drabness of their winter sleep. But were they all asleep? I think not. For scattered among them were several clumps of a plant with thin straggly stems which I recognised as those of the purple saxifrage; and when I looked at them closely I found they were covered with little flower buds. We could say, if you like, that they are waiting for the spring. But are they really? In recent winters they have started opening in February. And up here at 2,000 feet we would hardly call February spring. Yet the purple saxifrage evidently does just that.

Purple saxifrage in Cwm Idwal, Gwynedd.

WE LOOK FORWARD to seeing the great tides of the August full moon come surging up the estuary. They come always in the morning, the big tides, and by lunchtime they have gone as quickly as they came, leaving the wide world of the saltmarshes dripping and gurgling. Once more the mudflats lie open to the sunlight and hundreds of wading birds appear from nowhere to resume their interrupted feeding. By teatime the tide is as low as ever it can be and then there are other wonders.

All over one area of the shiny wet beach are the stumps of trees. They are not logs that the tide has washed up, but stumps still rooted in the earth in which they once grew. There could be no clearer evidence of land that has been lost beneath the sea. And because these trees are prehistoric, man has had long centuries in which to dream up wonderful yarns to explain how the sea broke in through ancient embankments to drown a fertile kingdom.

In concocting these stories, the local people may well have compared notes with their neighbours further up the coast. For if you climb that high mountain that towers up behind Barmouth and look north-west over the bay at low spring tides, you see another marvel: a curving line of stones called St Patrick's Causeway which reaches miles out into the sea. What else could that be for simple souls if not the shattered remains of a man-made defence against the ocean?

Submerged forest, Borth, Ceredigion.

ST DAVID'S DAY (in Wales it is Gŵyl Ddewi) came and went a week ago. It was cold and bright at first but then clouds came in off the sea, bringing showers of sleet and hail, and the mountains turned white. This was not the weather I was hoping for. I always expect St David's Day to be soft and vernal, perfect daffodil weather, but I admit it is often nothing of the sort. One Gŵyl Ddewi I remember vividly, though it is long ago. That morning our postman arrived with a large flamboyant double daffodil in his buttonhole. I dare say he expected some admiring remarks but instead I looked at his daffodil coldly and said that outsize daffodils are all very well but that, in my opinion, only the little wild daffodil was appropriate for St David's Day and could he please tell me where any wild daffodils grew hereabouts. But he could not. And there and then I decided to spend that warm spring-like day in search of wild daffodils. I went indoors and consulted the local flora but this informative book gave me a shock. It told me that the nearest spot for wild daffodils was 25 miles away. Fifty miles of motoring to see a daffodil. It hardly made sense. But in March it is not only hares which may act strangely. So off I went south to look for daffodils and after searching in vain for an hour I suddenly found them in a wet-floored woodland along a river bank, so abundant and crowded that they flowed out from the trees on to the nearby laneside, a heart-lifting sight under the still wintry trees. The sun shone through the branches, picking out bright yellow patches of the massed flowers. It gleamed on the shining blue back of a nuthatch, on the glossy black head of a marsh tit, on the bright green spade-like leaves of arum lilies, on white snowdrops, emerald mosses and the light grey bark of the ash trees. What more could one ask for on St David's Day?

Wild daffodils, Aeron valley, Ceredigion.

AN OLD MAP of this area shows how little change there has been in the last 200 years. Villages, farms, lanes, fields, a whole countryside: all are substantially unaltered. It is true that estates have broken up, that a railway has come down the estuary, and that a road has gone to the coast across what the map shows as a great trackless bog. But the bog is still there and the drainage ditches round it are much as in 1790. Only the River Dyfi has changed a little; it has wriggled in its estuary and wriggled unfortunately from my point of view because whereas it used to come curving in close to our house and must have been very handy for bringing a boat in, now it washes the far shore half a mile away. The river's old curve has disappeared under a solid level of grassy saltings intersected by winding creeks. But now that we know about this former meander we may come to look with more insight at finds that have mystified us hitherto. I refer to walls that are exposed at low tide deep in some of the creeks, walls that appear out of the mud at one side and disappear into it at the other without apparent purpose, suggesting the foundations of some forgotten city. Now we see they may once have been a lining built round the old curve of the river or are even the relics of ancient wharfages.

Dyfi estuary, Ceredigion/Gwynedd.

I SUPPOSE THAT among the simple pleasures of life by the sea one of the most ancient and enduring is beachcombing. It is pursued with zeal by all sorts of people and we can be pretty sure that very few of the thousands of miles of our tide lines are not walked along fairly often. There are two sorts of beachcomber. There is the purposive sort whose quarry is usually firewood. He can be identified afar off simply by the speed at which he scours the shore as if in fear of competitors. He is but a base materialist engrossed by the idea of saving a bob or two on his coal bill. But the other sort will bring home nothing of monetary worth. His joys are more nearly poetic, more anticipatory than real. He tells himself that anything that floats could come ashore from anywhere in the world and he sees himself picking up something really exotic. What he in fact finds, of course, is a cross section of the world's rubbish. Perhaps it is best for this sort of beachcomber to have an interest in natural history. At least then he may find a rare fish or a bird with a ring on its leg. In fact the bird-watching beachcomber need never despair. Many a tideline corpse has helped to swell a county bird list and one or two have been of species new for Britain.

Laugharne Burrows, Carmarthenshire.

TRUDGING THROUGH the moorland snow I came to the wreck of a house. It is a shepherd's house I have known for 40 years and it has been empty all that time. When I first saw it there was a roof on it. But time and the upland weather have pulled it apart stone by stone and slate by slate. After the people had gone a pair of barn owls lived there for over 20 years until the rafters fell in. Such has been the fate not just of this house but of countless others all over moorland Wales up to about 1,600 feet. Above that no one lived, for human endurance had its limits even in the harsh poverty of the 19th century. And as soon as conditions improved in the twentieth, humanity ebbed out of the uplands with the force of a spring tide and has never gone back. So the houses go on mouldering into the ground and already some are only names to be handed down the generations. There are many Welsh people, no matter where they live, who can tell you the old and often poetic names of houses their ancestors once occupied far into the loneliness of the hills. I am sure that many a sentimental journey is made of these old homesteads and many a photograph sent away to America and Australia much to the pleasure of people who have never been to Wales but who remember it vividly in their blood.

Ystwyth valley, Ceredigion.

ON A SUNNY MORNING this week I went scrambling along the unspoilt cliffs of Cardiganshire looking for grey seals. They are usually hereabouts but as there was none there that day I turned my attention to trees instead. Woodland of course is not a usual feature of slopes above the Western Ocean but here on this coast are some well known patches of windswept oaks which are a reserve of the West Wales Naturalists' Trust. No doubt long ago such woodland covered many hundreds of acres of the seaward slopes but the trees are now largely replaced by grassland and all we have left are these relict thickets perched very steeply just above the sea and doomed eventually to disappear as the cliffs very slowly erode away. The tallest trees are those highest up the slopes and they attain, I would guess, a majestic 10ft or 12ft in height. Those below diminish rapidly so that at the lowest edge of the wood, just above where the cliff turns vertical, they appear to be about 2ft tall, clothing the slopes like bracken, yet they may be some of the oldest trees in Wales. Just below them in spring you see cormorants perched on their cliff nests and the whole scene, the primal woodlands, the primitive birds and, if you are lucky, a few seals in the water below will give you as generous a slice of unspoilt nature as you can hope to find anywhere in the world of today.

Penderi oak woods, Ceredigion.

WHEN GEORGE BORROW climbed Plynlimon in 1854 there was a solemn moment near the summit when his guide, a local shepherd, ventured to suggest that there was not a higher hill in the world. Did the guide really believe this? Or was he hoping that this gentleman from Norfolk, impressed by being led up the highest hill in the world, might be persuaded to part with the most generous tip in the world? Whether he was a man of guile or not, that guide was certainly repeating a belief which had been cherished by local people, probably since at least the middle ages. I am reminded of Borrow because last week a friend and I climbed Plynlimon from the south – just as he did. It was a day of superb clarity. We looked across Cardigan Bay to Bardsey Island. South-west we could see to the end of Pembrokeshire. Round the south, the horizon was the uplands from the Preseli Hills to the Brecon Beacons and the Black Mountains. The south-east was guarded by the long black line of Radnor Forest. Away in the east were the hummocky hills of Breiden, with a glimpse of Shropshire beyond. The north-east was filled by all the hills and moorlands of Clwyd. Round the north stood most of the heights of Snowdonia except Snowdon itself, which was lost behind an indigo veil. On a rare windless day we ate our lunch by the summit cairn in warm sunshine. Then, just as we were getting up to go, we noticed three birds running about the turf about 40 yards away. They were dotterels, which had paused there for a few hours on their northward spring passage. No other birds have this strange habit of flying from summit to summit on migration, yet dotterels do so year after year. This was a wonderful moment for me. Though I had walked the hills for well over half a century I had never seen these beautiful little plovers before, neither on Plynlimon nor anywhere else on the terraqueous globe.

Dotterel, High Street, Cumbria.

THAT BEAUTIFUL PLANT, wild garlic, is now in bloom in our local woods. Not that it grows everywhere. But give it a fertile and permanently damp soil and it makes great sheets of cheerful green leaves and pure white flowers. It fills the air with a perfume that is not to everyone's taste. In fact it makes a few unfortunate people feel quite bilious. Yet some love it, as I discovered the other day when I ventured up the Torrent Walk at Dolgellau. By chance I was there at the same time as a party of French tourists and when they saw and smelt the rich carpets of wild garlic along the path, there were exclamations of delight. Who can imagine a group of English people getting quite so ecstatic about garlic? A well researched leaflet written by the local area archivist gives us the interesting history of the Torrent Walk. Part of a local estate, it was constructed in the first quarter of last century by the engineer who built the famous embankment across the estuary at Porthmadog in 1810. Right from the start, the Torrent Walk was made available for public use and so it has remained ever since, a delightful path under beeches, oaks, limes and hazels above a rocky stream that shouts and thunders in a gorge dark with leafy shadows. It is interesting that, more than a century ago, people were beginning to get anxious about nature conservation, even in wild Wales. A guide book to north Wales of 1878, when the Victorian fern-collecting phase was still raging, tells us that a notice board had been set up at the entrance to the Torrent Walk. It said: 'Private Walk. Visitors are admitted on condition that they do not touch the ferns and mosses etc.' It leaves us to imagine what precious ferns may have already been vandalised. The Killarney fern perhaps? It certainly looks the perfect place for that great rarity which so loves the gloom and spray of gorges and waterfalls.

Wild garlic alongside the Torrent Walk, Gwynedd.

RETURNING FROM a couple of days in south-west
Pembrokeshire I am full of the memory of the
extraordinary luxuriance of the wild flowers which,
always a gay show on the fertile soil of that corner
of Wales, have clearly been especially blessed by the
mild wetness of the past winter. Never have I seen
the red campion so huge and colourful along the
lanes nor the cow parsley and alexanders so
magnificent. Yet even these powerful invaders cannot
win every battle because some hedge bottoms were
spready with bluebells, wild garlic, hartstongue fern
or brilliant yellow stands of wild parsnip. But better
was to come. For the lanes took me out to the sea
cliffs; and there is nothing lovelier than the mass
display of flowers on our western cliffs in May, mile
upon mile coloured with the yellow gorse, broom,
lady's fingers, and hairy greenweed mixed with the
pink of thrift and the white of sea campion and
scurvygrass. The sun gleamed on them all and on
the blue green sea below. And beyond the sea
the offshore islands where the colourful flowers
continued. One of the special delights of these
treeless islands in May is their sheets of bluebells.
Now bluebells growing where there are no trees are
often claimed to indicate sites of former woodland.
But it is very hard to believe that any forest cover
ever developed on any of those gale-racked outcrops
in the sea.

Sea pink (thrift) near Solva, Pembrokeshire.

PICTURE TWO MEN in an icy wind laying a pipe to drain a farmyard muck-heap. Do you, from the warmth behind your windows, feel sorry for such chaps, wondering what they think about, or if they think at all, as the cold hours pass? If so, I wish you could have heard what these two thought and said as I listened. For they spoke of past things. Digging this trench reminded them of trenches dug years ago, once their spades had struck into pure sand, the sand our village used when it smelted copper in the eighteenth century. This memory took them back to that still older time when our stream was first dammed for the turning of a wheel. How many of the multitudes who admire and photograph our waterfall guess at its artificiality? Yet if you examine the boulders cemented in behind the fall you are looking at a work that stopped the salmon going upstream three centuries ago. Then I heard about the paved ford that used to be visible in the stream bed but is now washed away. And of landing-stages on the river bank and lime kilns and boat-building sheds of which no trace remains. And so on and so on as I saw the past reappear, like old buildings as a reservoir goes dry. And I learned, too, how much more there may be in the laying of a pipe than you might at first think.

Furnace Falls, Ceredigion.

SOUTHWARDS FROM HERE the land rises steadily to reach the windswept heights of Plynlimon, a mountain that is mother to famous rivers. East towards Shrewsbury flows the Severn. South-east goes the Wye making for Hereford. And down the steep western flank the river Rheidol reaches the sea in less than 15 miles, creating spectacular scenery on the way, especially the gorges and waterfalls around Devil's Bridge. The story of this river is not a happy one. Flowing through a region of abandoned lead and zinc mines, it has a long history of pollution and although it now runs more cleanly there is always the threat of poisonous chemicals getting into the water in times of flood or man-made disturbance. Then there are the reservoirs. One captures the river's head waters for a drinking supply. In a few miles there are two large dams for the hydro-electricity which is made in a power station along the lower part of the river where there is another reservoir. The valley broadens into what, until recent years, has been an unspoilt pastoral landscape. Yet even here, where you might expect the planners to safeguard the scenery, the extraction of riverbed gravel has been allowed to cause years of disturbance and uglification. You might think this poor little river has now suffered enough. But not at all. Incredibly, yet more gravel extraction schemes are being considered and if they are permitted they will industrialise a part of the valley for years to come and perhaps release untold quantities of pollution into the water. Then comes the final menace. Where the river flows into the sea at Aberystwyth a marina is to be created. Huge quantities of harbour mud, declared by scientists to be full of noxious metals, will be disturbed, perhaps releasing who knows what amount of pollution into Cardigan Bay. If only we could be ruled by planners who see a little further than the nearest pile of moneybags!

Rheidol valley, Ceredigion.

FOR MANY YEARS I have been a dropper-in at country churches but I often spend more time outside the building than in it. For churchyards are sometimes unintentional nature reserves full of wild flowers, birds, insects and small mammals which no longer have a home in the intensively cultivated land all round. Last week, when I strolled through a churchyard on the Welsh border, I found that on one side of the path, there was a stretch of neat but dull grassland which contrasted with the other side which was bright with colourful and scented wild flowers, a fine example of a meadow full of herbs that were common until modern farming practices destroyed such healthful and beautiful fields. At the end of the path I found a man at work. We chatted for a while and then he apologised for the untidiness of much of the churchyard. Weed killers were expensive, he explained, and he had been able to deal with only one side of the path. He indicated the patch of dull grassland with pride. I suggested to him that the wild flowers on the other side were altogether delightful and that after flowering they could be scythed without trouble for there were no obstructive gravestones there. But this he could not accept. For him, the modern tool for the job was weed killers and that was the end of the matter. To any passer-by, we were just two chaps talking amiably in a churchyard. In reality, we were the representatives of two different worlds. It is the reconciliation of these worlds that is one of the most pressing problems of the countryside today.

Green-winged orchid, near Llanrhystud, Ceredigion.

JUST BEFORE the long hot summer bade us farewell I went up the coast to Barmouth. I left my car near the promenade and took to the hills, which in Barmouth I could do very quickly because a mountain rises almost from the main street, so steeply that in 20 minutes I was enjoying a huge panorama over the harbour full of yachts and the wide estuary crossed by a long railway viaduct. I sat in the sun to eat my lunch while, several yards away, two adders lay curled a few feet apart, obviously enjoying the heat far more than I was. Fortunately I had no need to climb any higher for I had already reached what I had come to see. It was Dinas Oleu, the first property (1895) acquired by the National Trust, just four acres of rocks, gorse, heather and stone walls, a benefactor's modest gift but a memorable acorn from which so much has grown. Something else I wanted to see was the Frenchman's grave. Up there in 1882 was buried Auguste Guyard, whose story I have always loved. In France he had been a passionate champion of freedom along with his friend, Victor Hugo and others but, disgusted by the political repression of that time, he came to Britain and wandered to the coast of Wales, where he found refuge, thanks to John Ruskin. He lived a simple life in a cottage on this hill and was buried at his request on a slope that looks down the coast of Cardigan Bay. The centenary of the National Trust was officially celebrated earlier this year but I wanted to have my own commemoration. So it was that two sunbathing adders and I held our thanksgiving both for Auguste Guyard and for the preservation of a wild place, the forerunner of many that the National Trust now protects all over Britain.

Mouth of the Mawddach, Gwynedd.

44

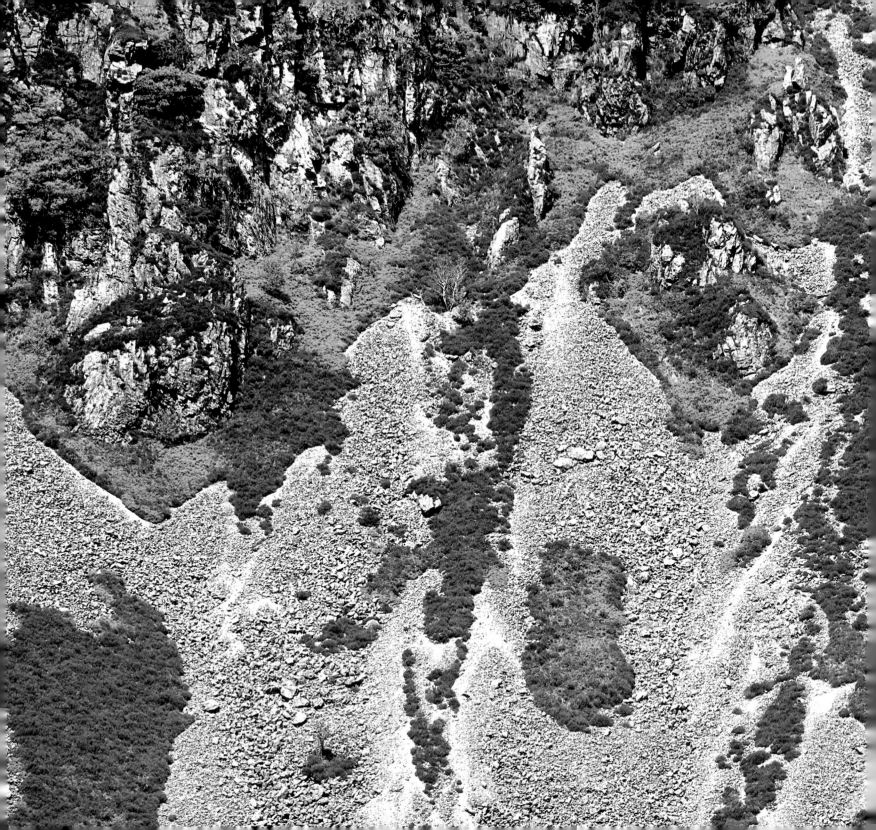

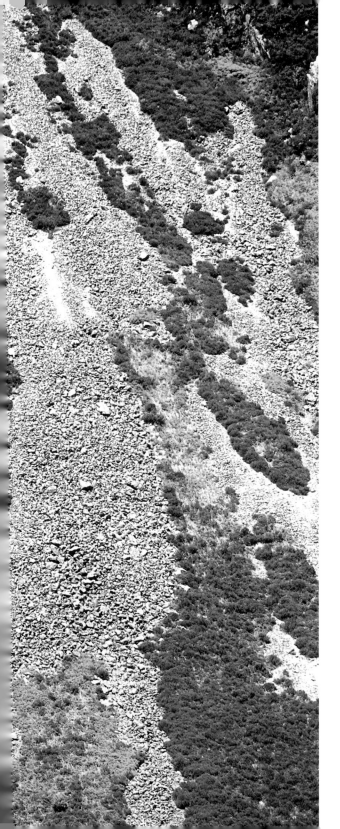

ON WEDNESDAY I pushed aside all books and papers and went for a walk across some hills about 25 miles north of here. Normally I am quite well behaved and keep to the footpaths, but there I could find no path to follow. For this was the great moorland called Migneint, whose name translated from the Welsh suggests bogs and morasses and my feet were wet in less than 50 yards. After a couple of very slow miles I came to a pair of shapely lakes that lie in a wild hollow overhung by great crags and screes. Perhaps someone ought to write a book in praise of screes. They are so neglected, yet they make a huge contribution to the majesty of mountain scenery. And as habitats for certain specialised kinds of wildlife they must be unique. Where else do plants and animals have to cope with such difficult living places as these millions of sometimes shifting little stones? From the lakes I decided to take the hard way back, making straight up the scree. And what a mistake that was. It was a scramble I might have enjoyed if the weather had held. But halfway up I was deluged with sudden rain. Have you ever been halfway up a vast scree in heavy rain? I don't recommend it. In the event I had to retreat, and came tamely back to the road by way of a sheep track. But though I had a weary plod I would not like this spongy Migneint ever to change. It is one of the last bits of wilderness Wales and as such ought to be cherished. And since it now belongs to the National Trust, all should be well.

Scree slopes on Cadair Idris, Gwynedd.

YESTERDAY BEING wholly blessed with sunshine I improved it, as people used to say, by walking northwards along the shore for two or three miles until I was stopped by the mouth of the Dyfi. So I turned into the dunes and was immediately glad, for I would otherwise have missed the little bird I saw there. It was a rather moving experience to be alone in miles of windswept empty shore and dunes and to have the company of just this one silent flitting bird, quite black of plumage but for a fiery quivering tail: a black redstart. These sand-dunes are altogether delightful, but only in winter. In summer they are too grievously afflicted by bipeds of the genus homo. Even now the sand has not quite buried the trail of tin cans and broken glass our summer visitors leave behind in grateful payment for the free use they make of our playground. But time and sand and the westerly winds will eventually hide horrors far worse than litter, we hope. I mean the hutments and gun-emplacements which were left here by an infestation of homo sapiens, variety militariensis (1939-45). I wonder if these vestiges of war, once buried, will ever come to light again to give future historians something to write about? I can see the history books of 2,000 years hence featuring a Battle of the River Dyfi as a key part of the Battle of Britain (1940).

Ynyslas, Ceredigion.

I WENT OFF on Wednesday to get to one of the great viewpoints of north Wales, that famous hill with three summits, 14 miles south-west of Caernarfon, called Yr Eifl, which English visitors have always called the Rivals. Though even the highest of these triple peaks falls short of 2,000 ft, its panoramas all round are vast. Northward it looks across Caernarfon Bay to Anglesey. South the view is all down Cardigan Bay to Pembrokeshire. Easily you see most of the heights of Snowdonia. And south-west stretches the Llŷn Peninsula with the sea washing both sides and with hills diminishing all the way to the end. Ravens croaked deeply in the upper airs and choughs called cheerfully in fields far below as I made my way up into the realm of bare rocks across many acres of heather which here and there was still touched with purple. I ate my sandwiches in warm sunshine on the summit cairn. But nothing is more fickle than the mountain weather. I had hardly finished my lunch when a cold cloud blew in off the northern sea and landscape viewing came to a sudden end. In thick fog I groped my way down a wild chaos of boulder scree and then climbed again, this time up the slopes of my favourite hill fort, that wonderful relic of the Iron Age, Tre'r Ceiri. Do any man-made walls anywhere speak more eloquently than those of Tre'r Ceiri about the Celts of 2,000 years ago? There is nothing like them anywhere else in Wales, nothing like these huge defences enclosing about 150 hut foundations. I had hoped to take photographs, but the mist, though now less thick, defeated me. I hardly need to tell you that when I looked back at the hills on my way home, all cloud and fog had unravelled and every summit was radiant in the evening sunlight.

Tre'r Ceiri, Gwynedd.

LATELY WHEN I took to the hills for a breath of fresh air I hardly expected a full gale of fresh air. But that is what I got as I reached about 2,000 feet on the southern slopes of Cader Idris and looked down on what, long ago, the artistic world used to call 'Wilson's Pool'. It was in about 1774 that Richard Wilson, who was born near Machynlleth in 1714, went up Cader and painted one of his most famous pictures. Even in reproduction this is a scintillating landscape of richly coloured hills and a dark green cliff falling vertically to the deep green waters of the lake. As I have done many times before, I tried to view the lake from the perspective adopted by Wilson but I couldn't find the right spot. I suppose the truth is that Wilson aimed to represent the scene in only the broadest outlines. For that was the way things were in his day: artists quite happily moved cliffs, woods, waterfalls, even whole mountains a bit to the left or right in order to make a picture more picturesque. Another difficulty is that Wilson has somehow managed to paint the scene too warm and brown and arid, rather more Italian than Welsh. So it is not easy to take a photograph of Wilson's lake that looks much like Wilson's picture though many photographers must have tried it. Not that it matters. What is significant is the part played by this and other Wilson landscapes in the shaping of people's attitudes to mountain scenery. If the public has learned to appreciate the wild lonely uplands of the world, it is largely due to painters like Wilson and the travel writers who were his contemporaries. Poor Wilson. His paintings may be worth a fortune now but he died long before his work was widely acclaimed. As someone wrote later: 'Scarcely half a century has elapsed since death relieved Wilson from the apathy of the critics, the envy of rivals and the neglect of a tasteless public.'

Llyn Cau and Craig Cau, Cadair Idris, Gwynedd.

BITTER TEARS have been shed by conservationists in recent years over the loss of the old meadows and pastures rich in wildflowers as field after field, even on remote farms of the uplands, have been drained and ploughed and converted into dull grasslands. It is true that here and there a few ancient meadows still survive as nature reserves. But this week I was treated to something exceptionally rare. I was taken to see not just a single field with its meadow plants intact but a whole sizeable farm which has been left untouched by the plough for many years and has probably never known even a whiff of artificial fertiliser. It was truly an inspiration to walk through field after colourful field, fragrant with a wealth of wild herbs which 50 years ago people all took for granted, but which now either lead a lurking existence on lanesides or have altogether vanished. These fields have survived so miraculously only because they belonged to an old-fashioned farmer out of touch with progress. But after him, if events follow their normal course, will come a dreadful deluge of improvements. These days we rightly take pride in the preservation of our ancient monuments, but here on the hills of Cardiganshire is something quite unprotected yet enormously worthy of being handed on to posterity: a whole farm complete with all its 19th-century fields. Somehow, though I know not by what means, such a unique property ought to be acquired for the nation. If money can be found to buy priceless works of art, money should also be available to buy masterpieces like this farm.

Wild flower meadow, Aeron valley, Ceredigion.

ON MONDAY a party of us clambered slowly up the eastern flank of Snowdon to look for alpine plants. The day was hot and we were grateful for the mists that wrapped around us from time to time. One of the pleasures of seeking Snowdon's plants is that they have a distinguished place in history as the first British mountain plants to be recorded in any numbers. A list of them was made in 1639 by Thomas Johnson, a London apothecary deeply learned in the uses of plants. He is an interesting figure in the annals, straddling the dividing line between old world herbalism and the emerging science of botany. Although it was high summer when Johnson climbed Snowdon, the whole mountain remained buried in cloud all day and he and his friends would surely have got lost in the mists if they had not 'obtained the services of a country boy as guide'. There has always been something of a mystery about Johnson's visit. Snowdon is a big, sprawling mountain whose botanically exciting localities are so few that a stranger could easily spend a day up there and miss all the choicest spots. But we know from his list that Johnson did really well, and must have got to the most rewarding places. So how did he manage it? I can't help thinking that although the credit for the discovery of these alpines is given to Johnson and other English visitors, they had probably been known to the local Welsh herbalists for ages but had never been placed on record. I wish we knew more about that 'country boy' who acted as Johnson's guide. Perhaps he had already learned more about mountain plants than Johnson ever was to know.

Moss campion and roseroot, Cwm Glas Mawr, Gwynedd.

IF IN the Welsh mountains you look for that rare but increasing bird, the chough, you inevitably become knowledgeable about the distribution of the abandoned mines and quarries in whose recesses the choughs hide their nests. Unconsciously as you stare down into bottomless shafts or explore gingerly with a torch along winding, dripping levels, you become mildly expert in the way ore veins lie in the rock. You begin to see things from a miner's point of view. You find yourself wondering why these levels and shafts probed this way rather than another; or why some lead to dead-ends and some go hundreds of yards into the hill. Having in imagination extracted your ore and roughly separated what is valuable from what is dross you still have to get it from the mountains down to a port. So along the valleys and up the slopes you create a whole system of trackways – horse and cart roads and narrow-gauge railways. For a few decades, perhaps a century or so, this pattern of communications weaves itself intimately not only into mining affairs but into the life of a populous upland community. Then the ore fails or prices topple. The miners depart and the rot of decay creeps not only into all their works but into a people too. Quickly a whole way of life vanishes, a life which to us who come after gets more and more shadowy, more and more forgotten as the years slide.

Above Trefor, Gwynedd.

THE RIVER COTHI in Carmarthenshire is a stream of much delight. It comes hastening from the hills to splash and cascade from one green pool to another, deep under steep woods of oak. Along its banks you will see grey wagtails, dippers and sandpipers and in its sparkling water there are many fine trout. Even more prestigious are the salmon which every year fight their way up from the sea to spawn in these well oxygenated rapids. But soon all this could change because the moorland from which the river springs is menaced by afforestation. These uplands have long been a battlefield. During the 1950s it was mainly an issue between forestry and sheep farming, the voices of conservationists being few in those days. That argument was won by forestry and now many miles of the hills are deep in conifers. Today there is trouble again because forestry still wants to expand but this time it is the conservationists, now much stronger and more professional, who form the chief opposition. They are worried that the spread of conifers has already destroyed far too much of the grasslands and peat bogs that were the feeding grounds of such desirable birds as buzzards, kite, raven, golden plover and dunlin. Besides, there is now evidence that streams rising among conifers soon become virtually lifeless through increased acidity and pollution by aluminium. So the River Cothi has become an important test case. Years ago I would not have had much hope. But today there is a new feeling in the air. Conservation is beginning to mean much more to people and our remaining moorlands and streams may yet be saved.

Tywi forest and Camddwr valley.

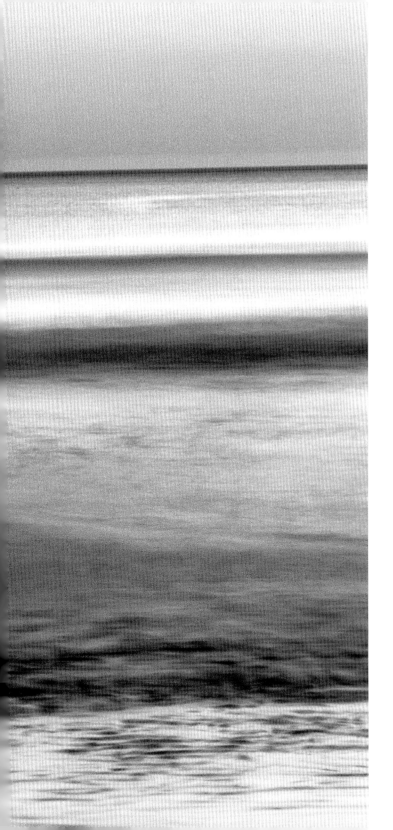

WHETHER YOU go off on a world cruise or just a trip round the bay, you take a chance with the weather. But last Sunday Father Neptune was benign as we toured the bird islands of Pembrokeshire with the Dyfed Wildlife Trust. Though the day began cool and cloudy, the water was smooth; and even rounding St Ann's Head, a spot notorious for lumpy seas, we had no problems. With red cliffs on either side we slid north between the mainland and the island of Skokholm. On the sea and in the air there were guillemots, razorbills, puffins, kittiwakes and shearwaters and they remained our companions throughout the day. Through the narrows of Jack Sound we passed our second island, Skomer, whose rocks are grey instead of red and whose birds are especially multitudinous. We continued north across St Bride's Bay to a very different island. While Skokholm and Skomer are flat-topped, Ramsey island is shapely and mountainous and above its great cliffs we saw two ravens and a peregrine. Our course towards the north persisted past a spectacular archipelago of jagged islets quaintly called the Bishops and Clerks. Then we turned westwards and headed for the open sea. Our ship, the paddle steamer Waverley, of Glasgow, now had several miles of serious sailing to get us out to lonely Grassholm where, in bright sunshine, we not only saw but smelt the gannets which spend the summer there in such numbers that from a distance they make the island look snow covered. Ever increasing, this gannetry is now second in size to the one of St Kilda, the world's biggest. From Grassholm we set course for home, again passing close to Skokholm whose now sunlit rocks were coloured with the bright red of sandstone and the brilliant yellow of those lichens which so love the winds off the sea. Back in the Haven we all agreed it had been a wonderful trip, thanks to the beautiful islands, the thousands of birds, a stalwart ship and perhaps most of all to dear old Neptune.

Whitesands Bay and North Bishop, Pembrokeshire.

WHEN THE youthful poet Shelley and his Harriet came to Wales like refugees in 1812, the haven they found in the Elan valley must have seemed the remotest place in the world, a paradise hidden among oak woods and turbulent streams. Shelley called it, 'a quiet valley which the tumult of the world may never over leap.' But what a dangerous thing to say about any place. The Gods who weave our destinies never miss that sort of remark. By the end of the century the house where the Shelleys had lived was at the bottom of a reservoir and soon the whole valley was loud with charabancs full of sightseers and has been ever since. Now after nearly another century the scene is threatened by a huge new reservoir to be built further up the river. Just think of all the traffic that will come up the valley then. The nearby mid-Wales uplands are the last big area of semi-wilderness left in southern Britain and so they would long remain were it not for big modern reservoirs. Already we have one in the north of the region and one in the south. Now we are to have this third one in the middle. Each will go on contributing its generous quota of tourist blight until the whole area has become a sort of country park. I fear this is how most planners want it though of course they will never admit it.

Elan river, Powys.

64

I SPENT last week on the very liveable North Wales island of Bardsey. I was there with fellow birdwatchers to observe the autumn migration but on most days the weather was all wrong. Not that it mattered. Islands are always enjoyable and on our first evening I walked to the top of Bardsey's mountain where, with choughs calling and playing in the air all round me, I watched as the sun's last gleams picked out every peak from Snowdon to Cader Idris; and when I turned round to the west I could see many miles of the Irish mountains, shapely and black against a blood-red sky. For the next few days, if we sat in the sea-watching hides, it was mainly to get out of the weather, for migrant sea birds were as scarce as migrant land birds. But there were plenty of gannets; and what more could anyone want than to see these brilliantly white birds, six feet across the wings, diving out of the sky in their endless pursuit of fish? Between the showers there was the delight of walking round the edge of the island looking at Bardsey's companionable seals floating upright with their heads showing, their large round eyes watching us with what always seems like intense curiosity. Our last day on the island was a halcyon one. True, we saw no kingfishers, but it was wonderful, as soon as the wind dropped, to find how many little migrant birds had arrived at dawn or soon after, commonest among them being that smallest of all our birds, the goldcrest. But it is not Bardsey's birds but Bardsey's seas that I will remember longest: the always changing colours and textures of the water; and those long mysterious lines which the tides create, dividing ruffled waters from mirror-smooth waters; and the white waves ever crashing up the rocks. Watching those waves I thought about the ancientness of time and how the sea eats into the land and how islands get separated from mainlands and how nothing in the world is permanent.

Ynys Enlli/Bardsey Island.

MY WALK on the hills last week took me past a
beautiful lake set in a large heather moor which,
thank heaven, is a reserve of the Montgomeryshire
Wildlife Trust. Then down to another lake and a very
lonely house which is now a sad ruin but which I
remember being lived in by a shepherd and his family.
Last week the only sign of life was a stoat hunting for
mice in the debris of slates fallen from the roof. From
there the slopes climbed across the treeless uplands
but this was not walking country. Instead the deep
heather made it stumbling, staggering, lurching
country where the only hope of decent progress was to
find a sheep track. I am no lover of mountain sheep
because they are so destructive of the natural
vegetation. Yet I have to admire the level paths they
have created, contouring across the slopes as
accurately as if they had been surveyed by
instruments. The sky was overcast at first but
gradually, in the far north, Cader Idris freed itself
from its clouds and here and there the sun touched the
landscape with a brilliant yellow light. I passed high
above a black peat-bog where little arrowheads of the
Bronze Age have sometimes been picked up. Then as I
climbed I came upon more signs of the Bronze Age,
not signs of their lives but of their deaths. These are
the great piles of stones they built in prominent places
to mark their sepulchres. I reached one cairn, then
another, as I came above the heather zone up into a
world of short grass and lichens where the going was
easier. My map told me that in a short distance I
would reach the source of the River Severn. But the
light was going, there were drops of rain in the wind
and I decided to leave the Severn for another day.

Glaslyn and Pumlumon, Powys.

I DARESAY yesterday's declaration of part of the Rhinogs in Meirionnydd as a nature reserve (complete with pine martens) will remind many regular Welsh tourists of how often they have looked at those shapely mountains without actually setting foot on them. So many admire that fine jagged skyline but pass on, being bound elsewhere. A pity, for there are few finer and wilder stretches of heather, rocks and small lakes in all Wales: ancient, shattered rocks, deeply fissured or broken into screes or sheared off in barren terraced ramparts so reminiscent of the Khyber Pass that the film 'The Drum' was made there. And back in 1188 Giraldus Cambrensis was equally impressed with the savage look of the Rhinogs; from the coast near Harlech they seemed to him 'the rudest and roughest district of all Wales'. But, like the majority of travellers, he does not seem to have gone nearer than that. If he had he would have found there rich traces of man's past that were one or two thousand years old even then: hill-forts, standing stones, hut circles, cairns, and ancient trackways, all the signs that man had formerly found the Rhinogs less inhospitable than either Giraldus or we have considered them. As for the pine martens, whoever sees one of those elusive creatures can reckon himself fortunate among men. I say this with feeling, having walked the Welsh mountains for years without ever spotting a marten.

Bryn Cader Faner, Gwynedd.

NOW IS the waterfall visiting season. At every spot that has a fall close to a road the cars stop, out get the people, out come the cameras, click, click, click, then into their cars and away they go. Sometimes they don't have it quite so easy. Sometimes they have to pay a little money and click themselves through a turnstile before they can click their shutters. But they evidently think it worth it, for some of these pay-as-you enter falls are the most popular tourist attractions in Wales. Incidentally, if it strikes some visitors to the famous Swallow Falls that Swallow is a strange name to give to a waterfall they are quite right to feel puzzled. The name, it seems, is a faulty translation of the Welsh but we are firmly stuck with it because it was introduced by Thomas Pennant, an eminent authority on North Wales back in the 18th century. Besides the few honeypot waterfalls there are many others, some really spectacular, hidden away in the uplands far from roads and comparatively unknown. Though not on any official list of nature reserves, they are among the last refuges for mosses and ferns. And if their waters drop down great cliffs they may be the haunt of ravens and peregrines or an even rarer falcon, the Merlin. All three of these birds like to nest amongst the heathery rocks at the sides of high cascades, too. Long may these mountain falls remain of little fame. The very best nature reserves, after all, are those which are not on any schedule, have neither visitors nor wardens and have none of those dreadful things called management plans.

Pistyll Rhaeadr, Llanrhaeadr-ym-Mochnant, Powys.

AS THEY sum up the profit and loss account for the past year, nature conservationists can congratulate themselves on the usual few successes and shed tears over the inevitable losses. I dare say in many regions the victories about balanced the defeats. But here in Wales, I feel that on one front conservationists had a very sad year, falling back in disarray before the combined forces of forestry and agriculture in the struggle to save the heather moors. The final decades of this century will be remembered as the time when the last wild moorlands of Wales disappeared. They started to vanish after the First World War when the Forestry Commission began its high level plantations, reaching as high as about 2,000 feet in places. Since then we have seen modern grasslands rising ever upwards to similar heights. Inevitably, the heather moors have gone on shrinking until today the very last of them are threatened. We cannot blame farmers or landowners for this. These people are under Government pressure and, worse still, are faced with the excessive economic persuasion that is engendered when big city money is looking for investments. Any sort of open country today is in great demand and high prices are now offered for undrained heathery uplands which used to be regarded as almost worthless. But why do conservationists make such a fuss about heather moorland? It is because it is one of the few remaining large scale semi-natural habitats left in Wales; because it is home for some very choice species of our fauna and flora; and because, especially in August, it is so beautiful and so fragrant. For this last reason, especially, the British public ought to be battling to save our heather moors, not leaving the nature people to fight the good fight alone.

Near Llandrillo, Denbighshire.

I WENT OFF on Wednesday to pay my respects to a pre-historic stone circle near Bala which I last saw about 25 years ago. But when I reached Llandrillo in the Valley of the Dee I discovered that I had quite forgotten my way round. So, a mile or so north-east of the village I stopped at a roadside restaurant with a beautiful garden and there I received all the guidance I needed. The sky looked threatening as I left my car and started up a lane climbing to the south. But then at the roadside I found a botanical treasure, one of those freak ferns so beloved by Victorian fern collectors, its fronds ending on a fork instead of tapering to a point. This I took to be a good omen and sure enough, as I got higher, the clouds fragmented and out came the sun. The road got ever steeper and more determined to get up and over the moorlands of Berwyn and soon I was standing in that ancient circle of 41 stones just as I had stood there long before except that I was now surrounded by grassland whereas the circle had been part of a heather moor when I first saw it.

I don't doubt that there was magic in the minds of those who set up this circle so firmly perhaps 2000 years ago and there is still magic there today, though of a different kind, the magic of being up there with the mountain wind in your face and of being able to look intimately across the flowing lines of the Berwyn uplands all along the south. Or if you turn round to the north you see, far away, all the peaks of Eryri. A good day, I thought, as I came back down off the hill and I had only one regret. On my old linen one-inch map of 1947 an ancient trackway over the moors is given its historic name, Ffordd Gam Elin. But on the modern metric map the name has been discarded. I wonder why?

Above Llandrillo, Denbighshire.

ONE DAY last week, tiring of everyone I met talking politics, I escaped into the green woodland solitudes that lie along the narrow valley of the Artro near Harlech. Mercifully in north-west Wales there are still many such primeval oak woods surviving. The Druids and their mistletoe have gone, but there are other wonders. The oaks themselves for instance. They do not grow out of the ground so much as out of rocks and the faces of cliffs. Vivid mosses cover whole patches of the woodland floor, they make green cushions out of the boulders scattered everywhere, they upholster the crags with green. They spread greenness far up the tree trunks. Where mosses fail the lichens take over, climbing to the highest twigs. Up there are also ferns with long fronds that give you a green wave with every breeze. I sat on a rock listening to a silence that was not broken even by the sound of a bird. It was that rare silence you get only in woods where the bleating sheep have been fenced out. For this is a properly cherished woodland, a reserve of the North Wales Wildlife Trust, a real wood as distinct from those many unfenced Welsh woods that are best described as pastures with trees. Outside this wood there is another threat: the goats which come down in winter from the hungry uplands of Rhinog. Your fences have to be really good to exclude those destructive monsters. As I wandered through the trees I reached a wild streamlet that broke the silence with much laughter as it came down through the rocks. I looked for special little ferns that love the dripping gloom behind waterfalls. In that ancient place I could have been living in any century since the last glaciers left their boulders everywhere. Then in this luminously verdant oak wood I had a few bleak 20th century thoughts about how our lives are ruled over by the sort of politicians who, whatever their colour and fine words, never have a genuinely green thought between the lot of them.

Artro valley, near Llanbedr, Gwynedd.

ON SUNDAY morning a party of us set off from here on a slow boat to the island of Bardsey. The north-west wind blew cold, but we were fairly sheltered by the land as far as the great cliff of Cilan Head. After that we were into choppier waters, and here we began to see those wonderful natural flying machines, the shearwaters, which always long to be out on the widest oceans and would never come to land if they could think of some way of raising their families out at sea. For the bird-ringers of Bardsey, the shearwater is the ultimate in migrants. As you can read in their current annual report, an adult ringed on Bardsey on June 25, 1981, was found 15 weeks later in Uruguay. But not by any freak had it flown those 11,000 km. To go to South America every autumn is simply routine if you are a British shearwater. After the chilliness of the crossing, the island welcomed us with warmth and sunshine. We saw the well-run bird observatory and its cheerful occupants, and then we inspected the rest of the island's houses. It was heartening to see, after many years of neglect, how well they are being cared for by their present owners, the Bardsey Island Trust. With the recent restoration of the chapel house, all the dwellings are now in good shape, and on Sunday they were all being lived in. A century ago Bardsey had quite a large all-year-round population. From now on it will at least have a happy summer community of holiday makers without any damage to the island's beauty or its wealth of wildlife.

Ynys Enlli/Bardsey Island.

AS IT IS JUST 50 years since the Government conceded that national parks might be a good idea, I felt I ought to celebrate by a venture into Snowdonia. So I went off to Dolgellau, where two rugged peaks, nine miles apart, look at each other across the Wnion valley. In the south-west is Cader Idris, which is immensely popular. In the north-east is Rhobell Fawr, which is comparatively unknown because it lacks both height and drama; no great precipices, no corries, no lakes. It was hot and airless in the valley when I started up the grassy, brackeny slopes of Rhobell. But it was a good butterfly day: meadow browns, ringlets, large skippers and small pearl-bordered fritillaries were busy all round; and purple hairstreaks danced above a grove of oaks. Somewhere a young buzzard made piteous hunger cries, and from a wayside thorn a pair of whinchats protested at my intrusion. I passed through a gate in a wall and abruptly found myself in a world that was richly purple-red with bell heather draping the rocks in all directions. And, mercifully, there was a mountain breeze. Hills began to rise up all round: Cader, Rhinog, Moelwyn, Arennig, Aran; then came Waun Oer and Ceiswyn to complete the circle. Above the zone of the bell heather, I reached the upland grasslands. Here the birds were meadow pipits and wheatears; butterflies were represented only by small heaths, that were having a great day everywhere. I got back into the valley with my mind full of sunlight and mountain panoramas. But my most lasting memory will be of those intensely purple acres of bell heather in the foreground of the view to Cader Idris. That evening it occurred to me that, although Rhobell is in a national park, I had not seen or heard anyone up there all day.

Cadair Idris and the slopes of Rhobell Fawr, Gwynedd.

THE OTHER DAY following a tip-off from a friend
I went to a North Wales mountain in the hope of
seeing that rarest of our mammals, a pine marten. I
chose a high perch among the rocks across the valley
from a spot where my friend claimed to have seen
the animal. I settled down to a day-long watch from
dawn onwards. At first the mountain before me was
a simple black shape against the sky. Then the sun
rose behind me lighting up the hillside's many folds. I
began to see clefts, scars, crags, and all these I
searched carefully through my telescope. As the sun
moved slowly round, probing the mountain from
new angles, I could see new hollows, new buttresses
being revealed by the play of light with shadow. But
no marten. By afternoon though I was still watching
the same side of the mountain it seemed a totally
different place from the one I had looked at in the
morning. For now the lowering sun had discovered
an entirely new series of ridges and hollows. It is
now of course that I should reveal triumphantly
how, just as I was giving up, I saw my first pine
marten coming through the evening shadows. But
no, I saw nothing. So was this a day thrown away?
I think not. At least I learned that there is more in a
simple mountain shape than at first meets the eye.

Y Lliwedd, Gwynedd.

I WRITE this sitting on a rock overlooking a pass through the hills of Snowdonia. The top of the pass is a level plain covered with what a foreign visitor might well assume are the remains of a lost civilisation. They are in fact the ruins of one of the many slate quarries which once made the Blaenau Ffestiniog district one of the slate centres of the world. Always when I am up here I think of Thomas Pennant, a pioneer Welsh traveller who came up this valley of Cwmorthin in 1773 and was impressed by its remoteness and solitude. The next century changed all that. The mountains were hollowed by mines, huge tips of waste rock took their place in the landscape and for many years the valley was loud with men and machinery. But industries come and go and now Cwmorthin is once again an extremely quiet place where on many a day the only sounds are the croaking of passing ravens, the cheerful calls of choughs or the occasional bleating of sheep. Gradually the old mines, quarries, tips and buildings are mellowing under the touch of nature. They have become objects of interest and wonder and are especially cherished by industrial archaeologists. Hill walkers have long enjoyed this valley as a gateway to the National Park but these days a shock awaits them. As they cross the park boundary, they find a notice announcing that planning permission is being sought to re-open some of the mines and quarries – a dreadful prospect for those of us who believe that national parks and their margins should be forever safe from exploiters and philistines. Reading Gwynedd County Council's notice we may possibly take comfort from the statement that 'the proposed development does not accord with the provisions of the development plan in force in the area'. The county council had good strong reasons when they originally excluded this valley from development. Let us pray that they will continue to remain resolute and not let themselves be forced into some abject U-turn. Snowdonia deserves better than that.

Cwmorthin, Gwynedd.

IN SPRING-LIKE weather on Wednesday I set off along the estuary. The morning tide was rising and a long line of grey curlews and black-and-white oystercatchers stood along a bank not yet under water. High in the sky three ravens, snarling and barking, were fighting a ferocious battle. One of them was a bird of our scientific age, for I could see through binoculars that bright red tags had been attached to its wings. A mile upstream I crossed the wide river by way of the railway bridge, thus transferring myself from south to north Wales. Here the river's wide flood plain was littered with the debris of recent gales and inundations: incredible numbers of tins, bottles, and plastic sheets. And tree trunks lay stranded on the top of so-called flood-prevention banks. Singing skylarks greeted the kiss of the sun as I made for the northern hills. Soon I was high up their treeless slopes with a view back to half the uplands of central Wales. Now the mountain wind brought out ravens, buzzards, and kites to circle in the upper skies, the kites easily outdoing the rest for gracefulness. I passed an old abandoned slate quarry where a raven flew furtively away from a huge nest of sticks on one of the ledges. In the afternoon I circled back down the estuary and retraced my steps into south Wales. By the ridge there was a red-throated diver in the river. Or was it a black-throated? I did not really care. In this age of ever more science I felt quite happy that there were still birds about without tags on their wings and whose identity was uncertain.

Dyfi valley above Pennal, Gwynedd.

WHEN I looked out on Tuesday morning and saw the sunshine and big white sailing clouds it looked just the day to revisit one of my favourite prehistoric fortresses, the one that looks up and down the verdant valley of the Dysynni from the top of the famous Bird Rock or Craig Aderyn. Had it been spring or early summer, I might have gone there to see the unique colony of inland breeding cormorants which are known to have nested on this rock for 300 years. But if by September the cormorants have gone away to the coast, they don't leave Bird Rock birdless. Long before I reached the summit of this sharp hill, I was being entertained by about 30 choughs calling and playing in the cold rough west wind and they remained my cheerful companions the whole time I was up there. As I stood in the gale peering down the great north-facing precipice, I realised that the cormorants had not completely gone in the sense that their stench remained, the reek that rises from seabird colonies everywhere. Perhaps despite all the winter rain, it is never quite washed away. A raven passed over croaking deeply. I looked down on a very red kite gliding by in silence. A kestrel hovered out in space level with my eyes. And the choughs went on with their ballet. I looked away to the sunlit sea several miles away but the best view was inland, the great bulge of Cader Idris rising sombre and cloud-shadowed above brilliant green pastures. Then I came down a hundred feet to where the slopes are crossed by the collapsed walls of 2,000 years ago. I hope their builders occasionally looked up and enjoyed the view as much as I did. But I doubt it. It was probably in fear and hatred that they sweated to build those defences against their neighbours, for the world they lived in seems to have been every bit as violent as ours.

Dysynni valley, Craig Aderyn and Cadair Idris.

ACROSS THE wild moorlands of Wales there are many miles of green roads, delightful public roads that no longer serve the purpose they once had. Lately I have been following some of them over the hills above Harlech and Barmouth. Judging by the frequent standing stones and cairns that stand near them these trackways must come to us out of the shadows of great antiquity. And they continue in use as trade routes in the Middle Ages and as drovers' roads. But in their present state they are much as the 18th Century left them when the last of the stagecoaches took to more modern roads. These days there are severe threats to green roads, now that farming and forestry are increasingly active in the uplands. But there is worse to report. On one of my walks I was horrified to find myself overtaken by two motorbikes and when they had passed I looked closely at the turf and found no sign that any motorbike had ever passed that way before. Yet, in wet places and up slopes the tyres of these two bikes had already done much damage. So, the danger is obvious. Mountaineering on motorbikes is now a worldwide sport and if we want to preserve our green roads and what is left of the peace of the uplands we need to keep these bikers off them. A green road is, after all, an ancient monument more dear to some of us than castles, or cathedrals, and just as deserving of protection. So what about it, all you friends of things that are green and peaceful?

Old Road above Bont-ddu, Gwynedd.

NOW THERE are birds' nests everywhere and the perennial fascination is seeing how they are made and how rigidly stylised they are. Blackbirds and thrushes exactly follow their ancestral pattern with ancestral skills though they have never been shown how. A willow warbler neatly lines her nest with feathers, but to the very similar wood warbler next door a feather is something strictly taboo. In the same wood a sparrowhawk builds her nest in a larch, a wide flat plate of a nest, strong and skilfully woven, and furnished inside with fine twigs. But this is not quite good enough. Before laying her eggs she feels obliged to prise a few pieces of bark off the tree and lay them in the nest. Nothing remarkable about that you may say. Yet if you go half a mile away you will find that another sparrowhawk has done exactly the same with bits of bark in her nest. And if you could examine all the thousands of sparrowhawks' nests in Britain, and elsewhere I daresay, you would find that nearly all the birds had duly placed such ritual offerings of bark in their nests. So other birds in their fashion take part in archetypal ceremonies handed down the countless generations. Somebody, I suppose, can explain it all in terms of natural selection. But it retains an element of deep mystery all the same.

Ynys-hir RSPB Reserve, Ceredigion.

FOR OVER 200 years English and other tourists have been exploring wild Wales. Some of the pioneers came by carriage and some on horseback but a few, like George Borrow, took pride in walking wherever they went, covering 20 or 30 miles a day, often in awful weather over trackless uplands. It is these strong-shanked striders who have always been my favourites. I love to think of them stepping bravely on their way, scorning all conveyances, moving about the world in the simplest and most primitive way possible in contact with Mother Earth and Mother Nature, the landscape always coming up slowly, so that there was plenty of time for them to enjoy it. It is a happy thought that walking is still something lots of people love to spend their time doing. As urbanisation goes on spreading, so people's longing to feel the wind off the heath increases and country walking gets ever more popular. So we can rejoice that last Monday was such a great day for those who walk in Wales. Ever since St David's Day the stalwarts of the Ramblers' Association have been beating the country's bounds, mainly at weekends, on their Round Wales Jubilee Walk, and this week this splendid trek reached a jubilant conclusion at two rallying points. Those going south walked the 11 miles from Caerphilly to Cardiff while the final stage up north was a walk of nine miles from Llandudno Junction to the promenade at Llandudno. In all, since March 1, 900 miles have been rambled and in a world increasingly cursed by motorways and the wasting of fossil fuels, an eloquent gesture has been made on behalf of the footpath way of life. When I remember the great walkers of the past I think always of William Hutton, of 18th century Birmingham, who first got up Snowdon when he was 76. Six years later he walked 600 miles from his home town to the Scottish border and back just because he wanted to see Hadrian's Wall.

Sugar Loaf/Mynydd Pen-y-fal, Monmouthshire.

THIS WEEK I've been having fun consulting botanists, the ultra-learned sort who write books of unimpeachable authority. My needs were modest. I just wanted a few simple facts about the wild apples that grow in our woods and hedgerows. So I took myself off in all innocence to a botany library, never suspecting that I was stepping straight into a minefield of controversy. Crab apples, I soon found, defy definition and make botanists crabby with each other. The 20 or so authors I approached could scarcely agree about anything. There was doubt about whether we have one kind of wild apple or two. Some even thought we have no native species at all. Others had very original ideas about the Latin names. But I found there was one fairly well supported school of thought which reckoned that we have two sub-species of wild or wildish apples. At last, I rejoiced, we were making progress. But then the arguments started up again, this time about how easy or hard it is to know one wild apple from the other. And now I began really to be lost in wonder – not at the intricacy of the problem, but at the total self-confidence with which the great pillars of botany hand down their pronouncements. One of them says quite cheerfully: 'There is seldom any doubt as to which sub-species a tree belongs.' But another soothsayer, just as eminent reports: 'We have been unable to make a clear-cut separation of the two sub-species.' Long ago the philosopher Thoreau wrote: 'The wind that blows is all that anybody knows.' After two hours in the botany library, I knew exactly what he meant.

Near Rhayader, Powys.

ON ONE stage of his famous walk across wild Wales in 1854 George Borrow set off south from Machynlleth and made for the hills. It was a day he greatly enjoyed, especially when it came to trying out his limited Welsh on the few people he met in that desolate region. And he was also interested to see some of the local lead mines at work. Those mines have long since closed, which is a great mercy, for they were killers of both people and wildlife. But today, instead of mines, we have the conifer forests which, it is generally accepted, increase the acidity of rivers and lakes and so cause a devastating loss of aquatic life. The forests are also believed to bring about a rise in the aluminium content of water, and this has serious implications for the health of all who drink it, be they people or animals. This particular area of the Cambrian Mountains has come into prominence in the last few years because the Government, trying to give itself a more verdant look, has declared it to be what they call an Environmentally Sensitive Area. So now the Welsh Office is handing out cash to the local farmers in order to restrain them from carrying out measures which would be harmful to wildlife. Yet, in the same area, this same authority is offering grants to help the planting of even more conifer forests which will certainly be destroyers of wildlife. It only shows what wonderful schemes can be devised by bat-blind politicians who, though they tog themselves up in green suits, can still see no further than the nearest money bags.

Above Eglwysfach, Ceredigion.

THE MUCH beloved, much climbed Meirionnydd height called Cader Idris was once widely believed (I am going back a couple of centuries) to be the highest mountain in Britain. Which Romantic traveller first got this strange idea I have never discovered but certainly Cader has come down in the world since then for it was soon shown to be not even the highest hill in Meirionnydd. But that did not really diminish its stature by an inch. With its long granophyre ridge climbing to nearly 3,000 feet above the Mawddach estuary Cader still stands up as one of the really splendid mountains of Wales, the only matter for debate being which is the more glorious view – Cader from the Mawddach or the Mawddach from Cader when clouds and shadows and slanting sunbeams are up to their sensational tricks. Here we have perfection you will go far to seek these days in southern Britain. And into this incomparable Mawddach land in the heart of the National Park there comes, with all the effrontery of big business, the Rio Tinto Zinc Company questing for gold and base metals and quite happy to despoil Eden with open-cast mining and who knows what other industrial obscenities just so long as they can exact some profit out of the place. We are hard at it conserving Europe this year. I trust we shall be equally zealous about conserving the Mawddach valley.

Mawddach valley from Cadair Idris, Gwynedd.

IT WILL BE many years before all the problems of access to the countryside have been solved, but among the triumphs of present-day rambling must surely be the coastal footpaths. The classic of this type is the trail that leads you all round the edge of the sea in Pembrokeshire. But now there are miles of similar cliff-top paths in other parts of Wales; like the one I followed on Tuesday on the coast of Cardiganshire. The path climbed up from a narrow cove deep between the cliffs and in a few minutes great panoramas began to unfold as headland after headland appeared up and down the curving sweep of Cardigan Bay. Through rocks and gorse and heather I followed the path for three miles; then three miles back with a blue sea always below me; and though the day was wonderfully fair, I saw absolutely no one, not even in the distance. I suppose it must be said that May or June are the best months for these cliffs, when the seabirds are nesting and the wildflowers make splashes of colour down the slope. But all the year round the rocks themselves are truly spectacular. In few places elsewhere will you see rock faces so terribly buckled and distorted, and speaking so eloquently of the awesome agonies the crust of our poor planet has always suffered. So maybe after all the best time to be on these cliffs is not May or June but at the height of some midwinter gale when white seas are raging against the shore. On a day like that the drama of the storm seems to go perfectly with the drama of those anciently crumpled rocks.

Llangrannog, Ceredigion.

GO IN ANY direction from this little town [Machynlleth] and soon you can be up in the loneliness of the hills. So, in Tuesday's warm sunshine, I went northwards up a valley that was at first dark with spruces. But in a mile I came up into a wild and sunlit world of grassy slopes climbing to distant uplands. I passed beneath a fine old oak wood which, higher up, gave place to a scatter of hawthorns. Then there were no more trees, only endless grasslands grazed by the quiet sheep of the hills. This is a silent and beautiful place, but was not always so. The 19th century made a violent intrusion here. Slate was mined deep into the hillsides and great tips of rock waste were vomited down the slopes. Then the industry died, the mining community disappeared, and now all that is left are the great barren spoil heaps and many roofless sheds whose walls are green with ferns. When in some future century the archaeologists dig here they will be amazed at the extent of the lost civilisation that once flourished in this remote spot. Two miles further into the hills the valley ends and your only escape is up formidable slopes. Even here, near the alpine zone, lead miners were busy long ago, but now their traces are getting faint. And that is how it is all over the uplands. You will not go far without coming upon old mines, deserted quarries, abandoned shepherds' houses, or far more ancient and mysterious walls now half buried in the turf. In fact, walking the hills is like walking across the pages of history.

Near Aberllefenni, Gwynedd.

THIS LAST HALF-CENTURY has seen a gradual move down of people from the mountain country to the valleys. But the years bring unforeseen changes and now new life is stirring in the heart of central Wales. On the east side of Plynlimon, men are busy planting forests; on the west the valleys are loud with activity as a great reservoir for the making of electricity comes into being. A reservoir here was inevitable. For Plynlimon, mother of great rivers, is a prodigious rain-maker. Her five heads turn their faces to the Atlantic clouds and often stream with rain when the world below is dry. And people miles down Severn and Wye wonder at spates in their river when they have not seen rain for weeks. At the north end of Plynlimon there is a peat bog full of ancient tree-remains, where, perhaps 4,000 years ago, whatever men dwelt there dropped a quantity of arrow-heads. Had they been of metal they would have quickly disintegrated. But these were of flint and so have endured. Even today the deluging rain washes one out of the peat from time to time. I like to think of the mountain now and then casting these arrow heads into the light of day to remind us how, beyond the long unfolding of the years, there were men loud and active here and trees growing where now is silence and the open moor.

Source of the Severn, Pumlumon, Powys.

LATELY I HAVE been observing peat bogs and especially the rate at which they are disappearing from the Welsh scene. Today, when British agriculture is doing so well, it pays to take on even the poorest land and improve it. So the demand for farmable acres added to the everlasting searching out of land for afforestation means that these days even those peat bogs which have always defied cultivation are being exploited. Does this worry anybody? You might expect not if the peat-bogs you have seen have struck you only as featureless, gloomy, forbidding stretches of waste land. If so it may surprise you to learn that even bogs have their champions. Naturalists point out that many rare and interesting plants and animals would become extinct if peat bogs entirely disappeared. And biologists, geographers, archaeologists are enormously helped by the studies they can pursue only in peat bogs. Then there are those who, far from seeing anything depressing in bogland as scenery, love it for its wild, wide-skied primitiveness. To them, as to the naturalists and the scientists, it would be truly criminal to turn a bog into just another field of potatoes. In the centre of Wales we have Tregaron Bog, mercifully now a nature reserve. But there are elsewhere bogs just as good which are in the gravest danger of extinction in these drainage-mad days. Unless something is done very rapidly indeed these other bogs will soon be all gone.

Cors Caron, Ceredigion.

THE OTHER DAY I sauntered for a dozen or so miles across the hills of south-central Wales and not another soul did I meet all day. And if I'd walked for a week I doubt if I should have seen anyone except perhaps an occasional shepherd. I calculated that I had at least a hundred square miles of Britain pretty well to myself, perhaps entirely so. Not a bad playground, I thought, for one man in an overcrowded world. Then another odd thought that occurred to me was that although the population of Britain is now five times what it was in 1800 and probably 25 times what it was in 1066, I doubt if you could have walked these hills in any previous century and found them so empty of men as now. I doubt if any age has found less to do on these uplands than the present. There are so many signs there of man's former activities. I do not mean merely the ruined houses and the decaying lead mines of a mere century or less ago: they are still names on the map. I mean those far, far older, nameless, grass-grown heaps of stones that once were houses; and the ancient roads and long-forgotten mines and summit forts and disappearing paths that are now but faint and fragmentary lines along the turf: the fading tide-marks of life that has ebbed long since.

Hengwm valley, Ceredigion/Powys.

ON WEDNESDAY I went off to climb what to me is the greatest of the lesser mountains of north Wales. It is the one that fills the skyline when you look north from Bala Lake and its name is Arennig. It is only 2,800 ft but because it is set apart from other ranges, it stands prominent in the view from many far off places. From the South and West, it appears tall and shapely, its flanks rough with tumbles of loose stones. But in the North and East, it raises great crags that give it true mountain qualities. So much so that George Borrow, who knew a proper mountain when he saw one, wrote of it: 'Of all the hills that I saw in Wales, none made a greater impression on me.' It was from the north that I set out finding no tracks except those made by sheep. For the paths on the less popular mountains are often more imagined than real, no matter how convincing they look on a map. Up and up I scrambled through heather and rocks. Above a lake, I found a gulley, which somehow found a way up between the cliffs and so to the summit. For once, I was lucky with the weather. The clouds of early morning had miraculously blown away and bright sunshine gleamed on grass and rock. The Southward prospect was immense across central Wales. But the hoped-for view of Snowdon was lost as the next surge of clouds rolled in from the sea and not for the first time this year I had to scuttle ignominiously down a mountain to escape a deluge.

Bala Lake/Llyn Tegid and Arennig Fawr, Gwynedd.

I WRITE THIS on the shores of Talyllyn, a highly troutiferous lake under Cader
Idris. But, I wonder, why so many trout and so large? Perhaps the good feeding is due
to some sweetness in the water that stimulates copious growth of water plants. And
maybe this sweetness comes down in the brooks that rise in the limy rocks of Cader
Idris which are famous for their kind influence on vegetation. And we know that the
liminess of Cader Idris is contained in volcanic lavas. And the volcanoes take us back
I never remember how many million years to troubled eras close to the world's
beginning. So a volcano erupts and the eventual result is extra-large trout in a lake.
But why a lake at all in this valley? And why indeed a valley? The valley is here, we
are told, because once upon a time the rocks parted in a fault all the way from Bala
to the sea, the lake itself being glacial and therefore comparatively recent. But nothing
endures; and the little stream that now gaily catapults itself off Cader and comes
rushing down to the lake half-way along the north bank must one day divide the lake
into two with its debris and eventually fill it up altogether. But by that time all men's
troubles will be over perhaps. And Cader, which saw man come into the world, will
only be a few inches lower.

Tal-y-llyn Lake/Llyn Mwyngil, Gwynedd.

LATELY I HAVE followed Meirionnydd's finest river the Mawddach from its source to the sea. It begins in high wet heather land but soon comes spilling over the rim of the moor as a stream that, when in spate as I saw it, cascades and bounces and spumes down three or four miles of a deep and narrow valley before it disappears into the forests. The middle reaches of the river down to Llanelltyd are wooded most of the way. This is the King's Forest, the ancient Coed y Brenin, a wonderful country of deep dingles, gorges, waterfalls, and countless side valleys all once full of oaks. Here about 1790, it is related, so mighty an oak was felled that the bards celebrated it in many verses. Now except for scattered remnants all that oak forest has gone and conifers have taken its place (with a fair amount of scenic felicity especially where there are larches). At Llanelltyd you come to a 'temporary' bridge (it has been there for years and shows no sign of disappearing) of overwhelming Black Country steel-girder ugliness. After that shock you are not even slightly surprised to find a caravan clutter close against the medieval ruins of Cymer Abbey. But astonishingly no one has got hold of the estuary yet. You can still look back from near Barmouth at flood tide at that perfect vision of water and mountains with, at dawn and sunset, the coloured clouds towering high over Cader Idris.

Mawddach estuary, Gwynedd.

THE NATURE CONSERVANCY COUNCIL was pleased to announce a substantial addition to its reserve at Borth Bog on the coast of Wales. Good news, you may say, if you care about the safeguarding of our last surviving wildlife habitats. For this wild and unspoiled stretch of peat – the largest of its kind in lowland Britain – is acclaimed as a wetland of international importance. But there is a very odd twist to this story of apparent triumph, as you can easily observe for yourself if you look across the bog from the main road halfway between Machynlleth and Aberystwyth. There you will see that a wide agricultural ditch has been excavated with the intention of draining that side of the bog. So we have the farcical situation of a government agency trying to keep a wetland wet, and a defiant farmer, unsympathetic to conservation, doing his best to drive it out. You may well wonder why we have a Nature Conservancy at all if it is so feeble that it cannot protect its choicest reserves from this sort of attack. Nor is this the only national reserve under threat. But let us not despair. Parliament has passed the Wildlife and Countryside Bill. So now perhaps we can sit back in wonder, love and praise as magic influences are spread through the land. Will the new act put fresh sinews into nature conservation? Will it strenghthen the security of cherished areas like Borth Bog? Or will it merely create new arguments, new anomalies, new absurdities. We shall see.

Cors Fochno, Ceredigion.

THOUGH I HAVE long walked the Welsh hills, I admit to deep ignorance about many of the man-made objects that are scattered everywhere. I don't mean the relics of prehistory, nor the remains of mining activities; these are well documented. What I'm thinking of are all the old house sites, the circles and squares of moorland stone, the long abandoned banks and ditches, and the trackways that lead you on for miles then fade away. Every one of these has a story to tell, but there seems to be little guidance available that would help us to interpret them or even to say whether they are 100 or 1000 years old. And what about those wonderful walls that go away up incredible slopes and then stretch out of sight across the hills? We are told they were built by the great landowners after the Napoleonic wars when unemployment was the norm and wages almost at zero. But is this one of the myths of history? For if you read John Leland you will find him marvelling at such walls as long ago as 1636. I suppose there have always been times when human activity has risen like a tide across the moors; and other periods when the tide has ebbed. I guess too that man has always felt curious about these traces of human life so far away in the loneliness of the hills. They are an uncharted world waiting to be explored and described by some gifted historian with ankles strong enough to take him or her across a great many miles of rough but beautiful country.

Above Trawsfynydd, Gwynedd.

THEY COMPLAIN, no doubt justly, that we do not use the railways enough. But in this respect no one can grumble about naturalists for they are among the most numerous and most persistent of all who find occasion to trespass on railway property. Botanists come first. For the plant-seeker a railway can be the nearest thing to heaven. Its embankments and cuttings offer him, all in a few yards, quite as satisfying a range of plant habitats, soils, and aspects as could have been achieved if our railways had been built expressly for botanical purposes. There are many plants on railway banks you will find practically nowhere else, so unique are their well drained, sun-baked, cindery, volcano-like slopes. A railway's flora can be so different from that of the country through which it runs that it can seem as if some deity with a sense of humour had come along scattering a rather fantastic seed mixture in a thin line straight across country. Then there are the insect-seekers and the birdwatchers. Many an entomologist's prize has been taken in a railway cutting. And where railways follow estuaries their banks are such obvious and natural causeways from which to observe waders and waterfowl that I have seen birdwatchers astonished at being turned off as trespassers as if it genuinely had never occurred to them that a primary use of railway banks was to facilitate the passage of trains.

Dyfi estuary, Gwynedd.

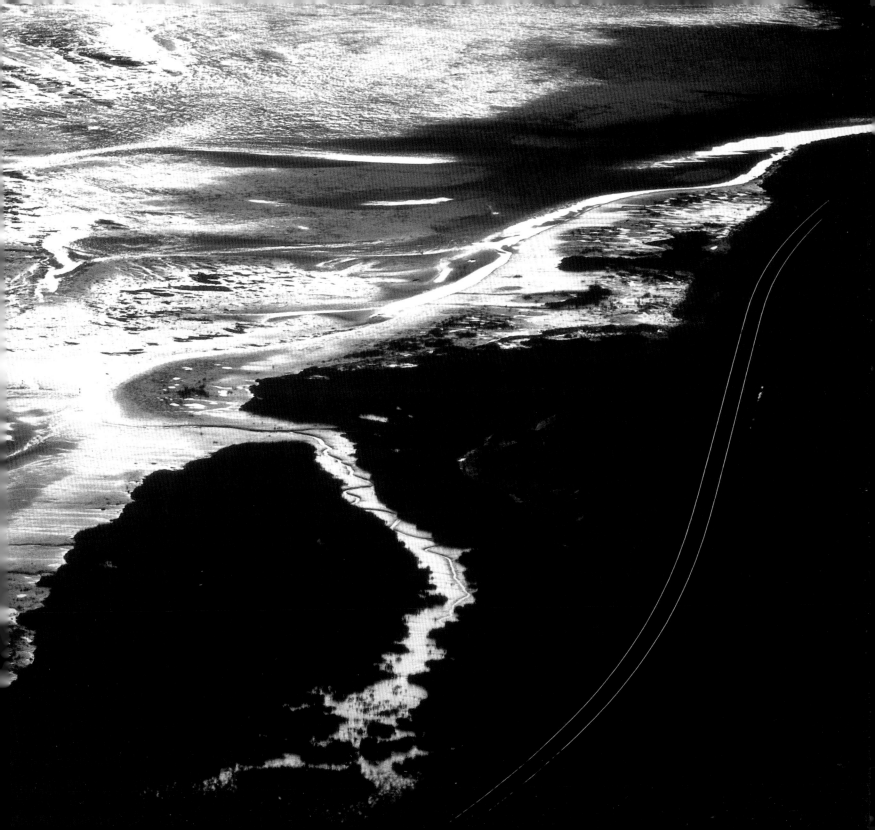

WHAT GOOD are mountain solitudes? Before the industrial revolution hardly anyone would have seen any sense in such a question. But today there are many in the world who believe that mountains should be preserved as a refuge against the machine. It is an idea which Britain seems slow in accepting. Even the Swiss, who seem hell-bent on plastering every square yard of their country with tourists, have their national park where the emphasis is on primeval quietness and non-exploitation. In Wales there seems to be no official thought yet of protecting the upland solitudes. (The creation of British-type National Parks could have exactly the opposite effect.) Though many of our vulnerable little mountain blocks are already criss-crossed by roads it is evident that some of our planners would like to see even more roads into the wilds. Hence this proposal of a loop road round Plynlimon that would strike into the heart of one of the remotest areas left in Wales. I certainly feel that mountaineers, ramblers, youth hostellers, cyclists, pony-trekkers and all lovers of the uplands deserve to lose this magnificent solitude if they fail to get together at once to raise the biggest possible outcry against this latest project of the tarmac brigade. The point they must be able to argue convincingly is that the motor-car, having already got access to so many parts of the uplands, should be allowed to get no farther.

Hengwm valley, Ceredigion.

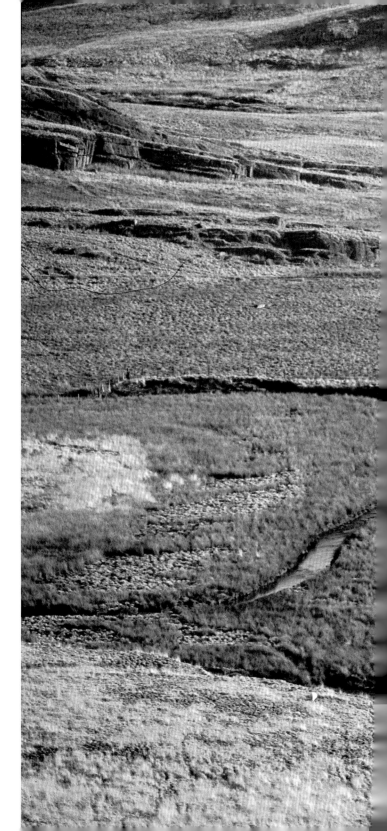

TODAY I HAVE HAD my annual clear out of the year's accumulated junk, a lot of it being the debris of a naturalist's days in the field. From my shelf have gone a collection of old birds' nests, some unsuccessfully pressed plants, and a few fossils and shells. But one treasure I keep. It is a long and shapely feather, broad and white at the base, tapering narrowly to a dark brown tip, a feather made for strong yet graceful flight. I found it in June on the floor of a steep Welsh oakwood. But it is not only for its beauty I keep it. I like to think of the fine bird it belonged to, the splendid and rare red kite. And I like to think of all the good country, all the folded hills and woods and streams the bird and the feather have flown over in their time. Then I find my thoughts going to other great hawks in farther parts of the world, the soaring silent eagles and falcons of the upper airs of other continents. I think of the forests and plains of Africa above which such birds in ever diminishing numbers look down on the ever shrinking wealth of wildlife on the ground. And I wonder: must man destroy all that? Ladies and gentlemen, I give you a toast for Christmas: To the wildlife of the world. May it be saved for all future generations.

Red Kite near Ponterwyd, Ceredigion.

8/9   I am not sure if the scheme Bill refers to here actually took place. Much of Pumlumon is now improved grassland, but its summit and some foothills and valleys remain semi-natural - indeed the Hengwm valley (really the upper Rheidol) has a feeling of wilderness rare in Wales (see also p126/27). Times and agricultural policies are changing, however. Research in the Welsh uplands is now more concerned with bringing back wildlife than eliminating it.

14/15   A victim of the awful 'Sea Empress' oil spill at the mouth of Milford Haven in February 1997.

32/33   As Bill's quest for a dotterel was a long but ultimately successful one, I felt that I had to include this picture even though it was taken outside Wales – and many years ago at that. In 1982 I was walking in the Lake District when I came across this gorgeous little creature. Not only is the dotterel one of our most beautiful birds, it is also probably the most confiding. Bearing in mind the unsophisticated equipment I was using in those days, I am still happy with this picture.

40/41   Following a concerted campaign by local people, and financial support from a rival company, the gravel extraction plans never went ahead. Now, ten years later, the Welsh Development Agency and Ceredigion County Council want to develop an industrial estate in the Rheidol Valley not far from this spot.

42/43   In Ceredigion the green-winged orchid is now almost entirely restricted to churchyards, like this one near Llanrhystud.

52/53   Not the photograph I had hoped to use alongside this 'Diary'. To the photographer's eye Cadair Idris is badly distorted in the Wilson painting and its perspective hopelessly wrong. It looks to me as if the painting consists of three elements – firstly a view of Llyn Cau from the north-east at about 750m altitude; needless to say on my three visits to this spot I could not get a decent picture. Then there is the grassy dome called Moelfryn, which the artist has placed in front of the lake although it is actually about half a mile to the south. The third ingredient must have been a generous helping of the imagination. It is difficult to appreciate how revolutionary it was for its time.

54/55   Arthur Chater told me the best wild flower meadow in Ceredigion was in the Aeron Valley and belonged to Cath and Ian Callan. I was surprised to learn that thirty years ago it had been heavily grazed year-round and only coarse grasses, docks and thistles grew there. By grazing the land hard in winter and taking a hay crop off in midsummer, the Callans have re-created a magnificent display of orchids and other wild species. Even these two retired botanists are unsure if the seed was windborne or lying dormant in the soil.

60/61   The Camddwr valley is smothered with conifers here where it enters Llyn Brianne. Important research was carried out in this area to compare the water quality and wildlife of afforested and non-afforested river valleys. The nearby Cothi is still relatively conifer-free.

64/65   To preserve water quality for the people of the Midlands, the Elan catchment area remains largely free of afforestation. It is now an important reminder of what the mid-Wales uplands used to be like. Plans for the huge dam and reservoir Bill refers to still exist, but they are now thought to be too 'politically difficult' to revive. Nevertheless, in a future where drought may affect the south-east of England, the possibility cannot be ruled out.

70/71   I was very pleased with this picture. Landscape photographers may plan their expeditions in great detail, but this one, at least, seems to be continually frustrated by the unpredictability of our climate. On this occasion a summer sunrise fulfilled all my hopes, and justified the early start and two-mile walk needed to capture it.

98/99   This picture was originally meant to be part of a series illustrating decomposition, but unfortunately I changed from Kodachrome to Fujichrome half way through. Never were the differences between two types of film more strongly demonstrated!

128/129   It is now far more easy to photograph a red kite than it used to be. Not only are there an estimated 1500 individual birds in Wales, there are now a number of feeding stations where the birds can quite easily be approached.

THE 'COUNTRY DIARY' DATES

The photographs are presented in the book as a sequence from January to December, and show the Welsh landscape through the seasons. The 'Country Diaries' themselves are in no particular order, and for reference purposes are listed below. The dates are taken from the William Condry archive in the National Library of Wales.

Page	Diary Dates	Page	Diary Dates	Page	Diary Dates
8/9	25.2.84	50/51	23.9.95	92/93	19.10.85
10/11	1.7.95	52/53	4.1.92	94/95	no date
12/13	28.10.78	54/55	28.6.85	96/97	2.9.95
14/15	8.10.94	56/57	21.7.90	98/99	27.2.82
16/17	1.2.92	58/59	13.6.62	100/101	19.8.89
18/19	5.1.91	60/61	23.12.89	102/103	1970
20/21	19.7.80	62/63	19.6.93	104/105	9.1.88
22/23	11.3.95	64/65	20.5.78	106/107	9.3.85
24/25	22.11.61	66/67	25.9.93	108/109	5.2.58
26/27	8.3.61	68/69	5.6.93	110/111	30.5.62
28/29	15.1.77	70/71	22.4.59	112/113	12.8.59
30/31	6.10.79	72/73	16.6.84	114/115	24.8.85
32/33	21.5.94	74/75	2.1.82	116/117	10.8.60
34/35	17.6.95	76/77	2.12.95	118/119	3.10.62
36/37	1975	78/79	11.4.92	120/121	21.11.81
38/39	17.2.60	80/81	9.6.84	122/123	30.7.83
40/41	12.3.94	82/83	26.7.97	124/125	22.3.61
42/43	3.7.82	84/85	no date	126/127	29.6.68
44/45	9.9.85	86/87	3.12.94	128/129	19.12.62
46/47	19.9.87	88/89	17.3.90		
48/49	14.12.61	90/91	12.9.92		